THOUGHTS

AF442338

PUNITH G S

Made with ♥ on the Notion Press Platform
www.notionpress.com

dedicating this to the person who's deppressed , dont worry I'm
here to listen you

Contents

1. LETS TALK

*Sorry to say but your efforts are not enough to fulfill the hunger of
the inner spirit
but i know you are trying your best
cheer up
have some good mood to understand
and enjoy reading.*

2. SHE(MOM)

"*She was the one who gave me birth*
She was the one who showed me firth
She was the one who taught me cirth
She was the one who's mirth (for me)
"

3. DAD

"*I KNOW you are literate but I KNOW you may not understand*
I KNOW you are happy for what you have , but I KNOW your sad for not getting what you want
I KNOW you have a dream but I KNOW you erased for us
I KNOW you are sad but I KNOW you are happy for us
I KNOW that i have to achieve something but I KNOW i cant
I KNOW i will say sorry but I KNOW I'm not gonna stay
I KNOW you love us but I KNOW you will get judged
I KNOW I'll die but I KNOW i too die"

4. CLOUDS

"When I'm watching clouds i imagine myself
With sun moon and celestial body
When I'm staring at clouds
I even imagine to go with flow like how it does
And even in toxic situations it still keeps on moving
But the day it's polluted more ,the day it cries the most"

5. I'm not me

When I'm not with me
Why the hell i should be with you

When I'm not with me
Why should I put efforts on you

When I'm not with me
Why should i be happy with you

When I'm not with me
Why should I care for you

When I'm not with me
Why should i cry for you

When I'm not with me
Why should i die for you

When I'm not with me
Why should i narrate you

When I'm not with me
Why should i love you

When I'm not with me
Why should i hate you

6. G A D (generalized anxiety disorder)

I guess everyone are facing GAD
If your not facing then u should be the luckiest or dead

Nowadays its a common disorder where everyone tries to be special with someone who doesn't even care about anyone and alsoo you have none to make fun in the run of life there is no return only the sun n the moon are common

7. DEATH

Death is so special if you know when it will arrive
Death is so harsh if you are enjoying life
Death is silent if no one's around you
Death is pathetic if everyone starts loving you
Death is surpise if you are happy
Death is aesthetic if you have a chance to choose how you wanna die

Death is complex if you are worried about your life
Death is painless if you dont give a damn
Death is terrifying if you get what you need
Death is confusing if you're in doubtful life
Death is funny if your depressed

8. THOUGHTS

1. I think even society doesn't care how we are , we just overthink of what they think!
2. Everyone are perfect untill and unless they see others perfection
3. Hate,love, importance, priority,value, cannot be expressed if its true
4. Just saw someone happy with bun and some unhappy with family
5. Everyone says shine bright like a sun , not required if you know how to glow like a moon with stars at dark

9. YOU

"You were never there during my tears

But you were always there in my tears

You were never there during my smile

But you were there always in my smile

I was something that u didn't need

But you were everything which i wanted as need

You were never there when i was down

But you are always in my down(bottom of my heart)"

Thank You

thank you for reading,huh i know everything has the end like that only

    i'm ending it out for today i hope every truama you are goin through

    will end soon as I

    may god bless you and love you byee!!!!!!